FROM THE FEVER-WORLD

POEMS BY JEHANNE DUBROW

WASHINGTON WRITERS' PUBLISHING HOUSE
WASHINGTON, D.C.

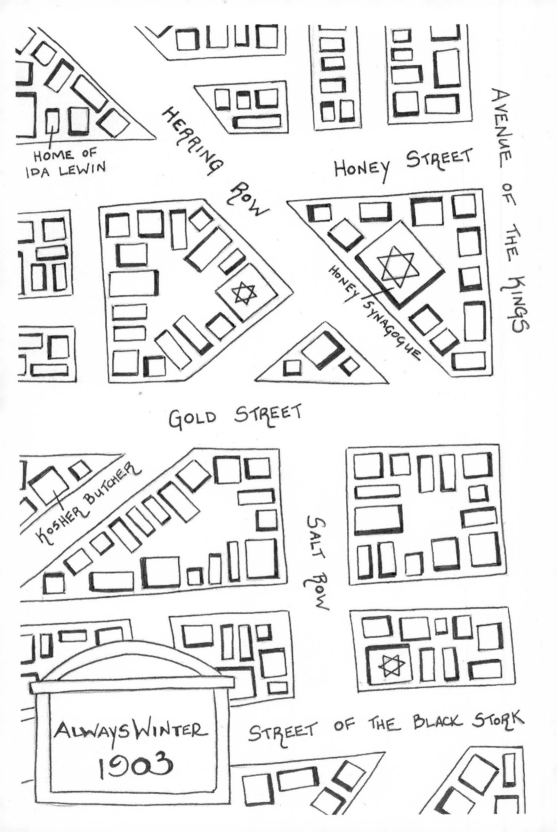

FROM THE FEVER-WORLD

Printed in the United States of America by Lightning Source, Inc.

Washington Writers' Publishing House may be best contacted by email at wwphpress@gmail.com.

Also by Jehanne Dubrow

The Promised Bride
The Hardship Post
Stateside (forthcoming 2010)

Library of Congress Cataloging-in-Publication Data

Dubrow, Jehanne.
  From the fever-world : poems / by Jehanne Dubrow.
     p. cm.
  ISBN 0-931846-91-9 (pbk. : alk. paper)
1. Jews—Europe, Eastern—Poetry. I. Title.
  PS3604.U276F76 2009
  811'.6—dc22

                        2009013410

Washington Writers' Publishing House
P.O. Box 15271,
Washington, DC 20003
wwphpress@gmail.com   www.washingtonwriters.org

For my two grandmothers,
Rose Portnoy and Johanna Dubrow,
who sent me the ghost of Ida.

CONTENTS

PART FOUR

Translator's Note
Acknowledgements
Thanks
About the Poet

PART ONE

Dear one, I saw it in a dream.
Avoid the red house in the forest,
beyond the plague of frozen fields,
potatoes hard   stones,
new carrots like knives that cut
the soil.
                    Curse the place
where birches grow
lacey screens, branches pressing
at the windowpanes   hands to gag
a mouth, as though the leaves
might stop a scream.
    doors hang open in the woods,
rooms crowded with ghosts.
I see my sister—
my father whispers at his prayer book.
My mother grips a candlestick.
                    their bodies
    melt away like wax. Beloved,
erase these visions of an evil eye.
Wipe the nightmare from my lids
                fingers soft as feathers,
your lips a fragrant salve.

Someone has seen the bird again,
that crane we call *December*—
December for the frozen rain
it carries in its wings
        We've heard *December* molts
black down like dust after a fire,
black feathers scorching where they fall.
     December's legs are bare
as branches in the wintertime,
its beak the red of poison berries,
each claw a rusted sickle blade
        we fasten knives
around our chimney pots,
although no bayonet can stop
the bird from nesting here
    laying eggs like monstrous stones.
Nothing keeps *December*, cleaving
through our dreams as though through air,
so that we wake
      faces scratched,
December's talons raking through
our hair.

Each year the chill creeps in,
        by June our eaves sharp
with iron icicles, our windows
rattling like teeth against the cold
        The ground won't thaw,
no matter how we press skin
to skin,   make a fire from
the friction we call love
This town called *AlwaysWinter*—
thistles remain needles, each blade
of grass a blade that slices
to our soles—how constant
the wind, the tundra in our bones

We've heard the ash-bird
soaring through the square—
animal that doesn't fly
with June, but caws the wind,
its prophecy the daggered beak,
its gullet overflowing worms.
It shrieks
    the reeds beside the river.
It is the gypsy charm
that can't fix crystal shards,
our father always dead
of heart attack
the velvet purse of zlotys lost,
the barroom talk turned nasty
and bleeding to the streets.
    after the shriek, the shrill,
we've crawled beneath a tree,
wingspan made of shadows
and choked on feathered leaves.

I am like the fire
from a Shabbes candle—
no larger than a poplar leaf
          barely luminous
enough to rustle
shadows from the wall.

How can I warm more
than my flickering self,
        blaze against
bad dreams, a breeze
which pushes back
the branches of my sleep?

Now winter,
        trees strip bare,
        my face remains
the only light. I shimmer
in the air and read
        reflections there.

To translate ripened fruit
to sharpened stones
should I devour my own tongue
or spit it out? Resign to knives
by offering my belly-skin?
Begin with fingernails
that hack ten crescent moons
across a lover's back?
Compress the heart?
What then? —a hallelujah
every time I snap red letters
like a whip, a praise-be-You
for blessing me with lips
to find the slingshot word.
Will I be saved by turning
pencils into nettle-points?
Oh please, command:
will I be saved by writing
with Your hands?

Before the wedding, a bride unveils
        to prove that she's the wife
her husband bargained for.
                the trick a father played
—Leah swapped for Rachel—
as though all girls might be exchanged,
one dented piece of fruit traded
for one bruised black

Truth is: the face remains obscured,
no matter how transparent the gauze,
silk thin   a whisper
in the wedding bed, white lace
composed of thread and emptiness.
        always we are veiled, even
in the sheets, our gowns only the first
of a thousand tissued layers underneath

Not every woman needs
a matchmaker to know
the rough dimensions
of her heart   cramped
        the space beneath a bed,
so tight only secrets small
as thimbles fit.
I store mine there—
            the metal taste
of my own blood,
how easily my hand discovers
the groove of skin,
the hinge, the sliding latch
                —I fold these
in the pages of a book, flat
as flowers. As for scent,
it is a dream of violets
in an open field, running
far away and fast.

little boots   little boots
—or so the love song goes—
I'll be the post which props
the corner of your bed,
goose feathers poking through
your pillowcase,
                the scarf
you wrap around your head

little boots   little boots
I'll pray without a minyan
beneath the poplars,
my trousers splashed with mud
          beside the road
I'll sleep in railway stations
              in public kitchens
where strangers slurp their soup
I'll wash the floors

little boots   little boots
I'll sell each shoe, walk
the calluses from my feet
I'll carve my finger bone
into a key   unlock
the doors you sleep behind
          My fingernails
will cut apart your seams

I cursed my body
while my husband slept in the clean
of his separate bed
                    I was bleeding,
a white cloth turning red
between my thighs—
                    skin unpeel
itself from the syrup of this flesh,
        legs twist like   ropes,
    my bones break into chalk,
            my belly shrivel
    a discarded fruit,
        each breast forget its milk
and the weighted shape of pomegranates,
may my arms
        my hands
        my fingertips extend like vines
but never reach
        my neck turn marble-cold
        my face turn toward Jerusalem
but never feel its heat
        my mouth repeat and then repeat
the prayer for the dead
        my nose fill with pepper, my eyes
with salt
may my ears hear only languages
they cannot learn,
        my hair escape the braid
        my mind misplace the name of G-d,
the recipe for bread, the blessing
over Shabbes candles
                —I cursed myself
            only to remember
that I'm both milk and meat, impure,
my woman's body treyf as pork,
my voice serrated, a filthy knife.

[version one]

12

Who obliterates the body?
—my husband, when I bleed,
and he cannot peel my skin
like a windfall apple knocking
from the tree or the split
pomegranate,
     can't twist my leg to ropes,
         my twig arms,
    the vines of fingertips,
  can't reach for the marble
of my neck, this carved surface
that is said to be my face,
  can't warm himself
against my mouth, but cools
as though preparing for a death,
the loss of spice after a thousand
years of eating, and all the red
forgotten names, the swallowed light—
He hates the body, draws back,
then raises high the knife.

           [version two]

the body is a curse
that tastes of fruit
and the body is a fruit
that splits apart
and the parts are rope
to strangulate the tree
and the tree has stretched itself
to reach the stone
and the marble has a face
which cannot smile,
the smile never warms,
and the mouth is animal
forgotten how to eat,
and the hunger
is divided by a dirty knife

[version three]

I come back from the bath
          my body kosher
     clean like a new china plate,
your hands on me   delicate,
          as though my wrists
are goblet stems, blown glass
that shatters at the feast.
You swallow from my palms
with thirst that comes from fasting.
                    I will not break,
beloved, although you curve
into a basket and carry me
          not an egg
to crack, or bitter herbs,
or the bowl of salt water to dip
your fingers in   I'm crumbs
of bread that fall before Pesach
and rot forgotten in the dark.

            to be studied, the way
my husband drags a fingertip
from right to left across his siddur,
            black letters fluttering
like eyelashes against
the softest flesh—let him be
a scholar and I the text,
speak me on Yom Kippur
while the congregation bows
and sways, voices praying me,
myself the blessing when they pour
the wine   myself
the motsi said before a meal,
            let the rebbe teach the right
pronunciation for myself,
let there be a midrash to the mole
that punctuates my breast,
a hermeneutics of the scar
so pale across my palm,
still legible though the kitchen blade
inscribed me   years ago,
   let my husband read what men,
the wisest men in the village
have written on my face,
the vellum of my name

I believe in the body's power
to hurt itself—
        bury the crescent moons
of nail clippings behind the house,
                unravel strands of hair
from the brush's spines
then float them down the Vistula,
                   bless the eyelash
fallen from the cheek, the bead
of blood   poisonous berry
squeezed from the fingertip,
the scab, brown as a forest mushroom
which peels itself back to bare
the pink beneath, as though a petal
of the flower-wound
—no mistake that evil is named
for the eye, our own gaze blue
and ominous as water,
        pupil black,   so deep
we cannot see its end, a well
that tunnels to the buried earth.

PART TWO

If beets complain, they say,
the root of me is blood.
Although you wish me pale
potato-white
   weeping onion-tears,
I can't hide my heart despite
a pointed tip that jabs
the earth.
I end in sprays of green.
      Why not look past
my roughened skin,
the dirt I'm buried in?
           Peel me.
      I take your spice.
My neighbors stand a pinch
of salt but little else,
   their thousand eyes
held shut against the world
I have no eyes to keep
you out. Squeezed dry
then tossed into a heap,
I'm vegetable with rot.
It's mine, this sacrifice
that stains your knife.
I gleam   I hemorrhage
inside your hunger-dreams.

At Purim, an angel dances
on the cobblestones.
She's from the world-to-come,
except for her new shoes
        the soles unmarked,
the kidskin leather still unscratched.
Perhaps the little daughter goes
to shul to celebrate HaShem,
his work hidden behind a mask
of lucky accidents. She cries
thank you
        a history of close calls.
Each time the rebbe says *Haman*,
she shakes a noisemaker,
until its hiss obliterates the name.
If only every evil man
were crushed by children's shouts,
        his shame delighted in
like treats, his rule trampled
beneath the dancers in the street.

After fasting I'm thinner than
a broth, so watered down
      the taste is meatier
in memory than on the tongue.
            Perhaps
this is how holiness begins—
without dumplings floating
like geese across the surface,
without carrots ringed
like ancient trees,
      without the lace of parsley
        —I am clear liquid
ladled from the pot and spooned
into the bowl that opens as a mouth
      I am the paradox
of spice exchanged for plenty,
      the thickened soup
exchanged for clarity, the fullness
that begins with emptiness

                        winters in Poland,
the Sabbath bride   arrives
by four, adorned in her greatcoat
of snow and sleet, the wind sharpening
its nails against the roof.
How welcome the candles are—
            two heats shielded
between my hands, blue shadow-birds
that light the walls to shut
                    December out.
Their wings can warm the room
or be extinguished with a word.
In every home: two braided loaves,
meat stews slow-cooking seven hours.
The twilight flickers like a torch.
            someone should write a book
which chronicles
the taste of kugel on the tongue.
Start with blessings and end
with melodies that don't endure.

                        [version one]

Shabbes is a bride,
her gown embroidered snow.
The wind desires her, its breath
turned crystal on the windowpanes,
its nails   sleet against the roof.
How welcome   the candles—
small heats nesting in between
my hands, blue birds in shadow.
Their wings set fire to the room
          or else they're snuffed with words.
In every home: two breads, a stew
so cooked it makes an alchemy.
I want to write a book
which tastes like kugel on the tongue.
I want to bless this place and all
the melodies that sputter out.

                          [version two]

Right ear fell to the ground
and heard the Vistula
        left ear fell near
my mother's town
now smudged from maps.
Ten toes were scattered
in a minor key, the sharp
paprika steps of romany
            my nose dropped
to the steppe, smelling
potato vowels and cabbage
consonants. What else?
My eyelashes fluttered
past tall ships to groves
where they caressed
the velvet peels of fruit.
Don't ask about my heart—
it beats   not with itself
but with the places tasting
most of rest.

forewarned, we spent the night
crouched in a field of corn,
          (we have become guilty)
uneasy among the ears,
not knowing day would bring
worse noises than the green
          (we have caused wickedness)
stalks swaying in the dark
               (we have sinned willfully)
like one, one body moved
as if thinking one thought

the wind threshed through the field,
a scythe, invisible
except to ghosts and those
                    (we have rebelled, provoked)
not long from death, the ones
          (we've acted wantonly)
already dried to husks.
The dirt crunched underfoot.
And moonlight showed the corn
          (you've let us go astray)
silk glinting   Slavic hair

I've heard that Polish wives cook beets
into a broth the red of hemorrhage.
They fill white bowls with dumplings
in the shape of shrunken ears,
molding pastry that looks like lobe
and auricle   Consider ears (to hear
one's own devouring before it comes),
they know the scrape of metal in the bowl,
pale cochleae that float across the soup.
        poor things can't seal themselves
against the sound but roll, swirling
past a spoon. A meal for cannibals—
with such an audience below,
I lose the taste for flesh and dough.

Once I held a painted miniature
of the Madonna,
      her face so small she fit
inside my fist, but still left room
to hide two zloty coins
that I threw into the fountain,
                  a pinch
of poppy seeds   for feeding finches,
a psalm to read beside
the rebbe's tomb,
         where every word
turns stone or plumes into a bird—
silhouette and light, both fall and flight.

I watch the Polish women sell
their wares—ham hocks
and hooves   blood sausages
strung up like strands of beads,
cakes black with poppy seeds,
and rows of amber honey jars
where warmth turns crystal,
        refracting like the stained glass
of a church, each liquid ray
so yellow-sweet
I draw my finger through the light.

What freedom in this commerce.
A woman brushes up
against a man, coins dropping palm
to palm, their contact quick
as breath   and treyf as pork.
There are evenings when I dream
the taste of bacon, the soft whisper
of a stranger's hand on mine.
His words are salt and sugar
kosher   but only in
the sacred law of my own skin.

late summertime,
when raspberries grow fuzz,
white mold where sweetness was
a month before, I buy
Italian plums—each one
a concentrated knot
a fist of purple
and just below, green flesh
that glows like fireflies
illuminating dusk.
Small plums.
I never eat enough. My thumbs
split every fruit along the cleft,
that symmetry of halves,
only the pit still left,
a plate of stones where plums
had been, my fingers sore
and bitten, my belly rounded
like a plum
as if I have myself become
the seed, the source, the juice
of appetite.

On Rosh Hashanah, I try
the trick of making honey cake—
not walnuts mixed with dough
which Mamme recommends,
           candied orange peel,
not apples from the peasant's field,
or cloves and cinnamon, scented
as a Shulamite
—the trick, as with all women's work,
is disappointment,
                an old letter
tied shut with silk
then stitched into my apron hem,
each sentence syrup promises,
the words *my dearest love*
                    like fat
dissolving in the mouth to leave
an oily taste,
and every last *goodbye*, a pinch
of salt stirred in the recipe
        to make it sweeter,
but with a bitterness that sticks
like honey on the tongue.

PART THREE

In the fever-world, my dearest,
our hands aren't clean
for very long, the brambles
biting in our palms,
deep thorns across our life lines—
      here, even the shrub
surrendering fruit to the picker
resents the sacrifice and wants
its juices given back in blood.
      if you are hungry, starve yourself.
Make a desert of your thirst.
Don't fall asleep
            Here, my dearest,
there's only wilderness where fields
should be, only the blackberries
concealing knives,
            cherries pitted with buckshot
to choke the unsuspecting throat,
and peaches whose centers hold
dark stones of cyanide.

I have swaddled the baby
in a blanket—
wrapped like a cabbage roll,
she's warm, as though from baking,
her breath sweet cinnamon
and raisins,   her voice
        the burble of a meal
that's close to done
                —I would eat her,
hold her again in the dark oven
of my belly,
where the air is tangible with heat.
There, she could not catch a chill
or a fever that burns
        all juices from her mouth,
her face turned wax paper,
her body charred but cold
inside its layers, unmoving
and untouchable   as death

I dream the myth of men
      who lead the living
to the dead.   like potatoes,
    mute for what they know
for where they've stood,
planted in the earth. They've bled
their secrets in the purpled
creases of a cabbage.
No answers when they're asked
about the terminus,
only a shrug   tongueless
    and indecipherable,
as if the spirits pulled
all language from its roots,
left dirt   some chimney soot
  and fingerprints behind,
tunnels collapsing in the mind.

This country is a dollhouse,
a shadow box of birch trees
carved with hearts,   displays
of small-scale chestnuts
rotting to be picked.
            childhood is a church
where no one comes to light
a votive for the glass-eyed dead,
the collection plate
an empty hand. The ground
is papered with a thousand flakes
of cut-out snow.
Hopscotchland, I can't escape.
I can't wake up from ash
which mountains in my memory
to fill the porcelain spaces
of my mouth.

                              [version one]

In the dollhouse world
even the trees can fit
inside a box,
a whole life small enough
        to hold. Childhood
is a church in miniature,
a forgotten toy.
The Hopscotchland is ash,
a thousand paper flakes,
a mountain made of jacks,
a game of catch
release   and catch again

[version two]

I think she must be Death—
the one who knocked today,
a stranger with her box
        of poisoned sweets
to sweeten me.
The locks screeched
like a child when I let
her in. They knew her voice,
wet and green as snot.
The hallway knew
her too. How could it not?
She dragged her shoes across
the knots, as if her soles
had memorized the wood
            as if her feet
or feet like hers had stood
in that same spot before.
I took her sweets but watched
her sharpened fingernails.
        A treat she hissed.
I choked on chocolate filled
with wine, purple-black
as iodine.

Tonight   I am remembering
my baby's feet each toe
          a pink pink currant,
her soles soft dough, clean
from never having known
the world of dirt.
Tell me, should I wish
my child preserved in a bottle,
forever sweetened there,
          her tiny thumb held
like a stopper to the mouth?
          or should a mother dream
of rot, instead?   an airtight jar
may mean the opposite of death,
          summer berries kept
always fresh, fruit poised
behind the glass but never picked

Some claimed
the farmer made his soil bleed,
poured pomegranate juice
among the seeds. A stone
flashed liquid red like blood
on clay.
Some claimed the ground
was a woman's wound
now draining clean of birth
and afterbirth and even
the dried-up memory
of pain

[version one]

The farmer bled his field, split
earth apart like the casing
of a pomegranate. Red stones
unpeeled themselves from dirt,
rubies where only rocks
should grow.
Is this the landscape healing
from a wound?
        —A woman
trying to forget the birth
she never wanted,
the burden she pushed
and pushed away,
like a piece of fruit
and she without
an appetite.

                [version two]

The field was furrowed like the space
between a woman's legs. It bled
so that the fallow birthed
the purity of dirt
          and undiscovered stones—
a resting place for seeds
and rubies made to taste
like fruit.

                    [version three]

In the city of machines,
the trolley track transforms
into a river. I follow it,
the dirge of humming rails
    more liquid-resonant
than any Vistula
There's meaning in metal,
although the books proclaim
that only stone can answer
to our exile   only glass
is vessel for the soul.
I do not weep beside
this Babylon or drown
the way my mother might
have done. I am the modern voice
and this my lamentation,
    a current borne
on electricity and steel

I've heard it said
embalming loss
is what the goyim do,
     each grief
soaked in formaldehyde,
like jars of bone
to hold up to the light.
They build a shrine
and call it memory.
    choose life,
the Torah warns,
because the choice
     (swift
as walking through
a darkened passageway)
divides   us from
the steady cold of earth.
We lock our dead
in pine, let buried ones
stay buried.

My mind grew quiet
like a house at dusk,
    rooms black, except
for moonlight stroking walls.
Then sleep unlocked the door.
When sleep appeared, removed
its robe, and wrapped its arms
around my neck
whispering *plunder* in my ear,
I even welcomed death
to snuggle down. When death
sistered itself to sleep,
not brusque, but coy and clever
as the start of fall—signaled
by a first vermilion leaf,
a chill against my cheek—
then the sky opened like a box
too full of diamond stars.
When the stars reduced all nights
    to a jar   stones,
gray pebbles in a hand,
then my mind could settle in
its house   and still.

only the skeleton
of rooms, absences
where walls once stood,
like bits of life
remembered on the bone.
White plaster swirled.
Daylight fell differently
across the floor-no-longer-floor,
girder and joist now anatomy.
What is a house with all
partitions gone? A shell,
a skull that forms itself
around the shape of fullness
but not the weight of it,
a rib cage ready to inflate,
      expanding through
a furnace blast of sound.
No breath. A body needs
the chambered heart,
its atria, to hold
blood-worlds apart.

The missing child won't
be found, although I claw
through every hidey-hole,
each spot a baby crawls
into to die. She's crying
there inside the ground,
          sucking the milk
of nightmares mothers make,
when they have nothing left
to give   I feel
her growing fat although
I cannot hold her fingers
anymore, those tiny ropes
that used to choke my thumbs,
     my own hands turned
to white, unfeeling stones.

Those women who sit shiva
for babies never seeded—
each worries the hollow
underneath her ribs,
feeling at skin now loose
        which once was full
as a ripened plum
                and round.
The body's memory
is worse than any hunger.
        an appetite
for food that won't be found,
the search for an impossible fruit
in winter's cabinet,
a thirst so deep the tongue
will recreate the taste of juice.

Someday we'll say
remember when,
as if remembering
were a swift
and easy gesture
like scooping sand
from the shallow bed
of a stream—
our hands cupping
clear water or a fish
so miniscule
it could be a pendant
on a silver chain
        —even
the sediment
won't cut our palms,
although each grain
is certainly the birth
of glass, each mote
the blinding of
our   eyes
which should be shut,
     each blink
an effort to forget
and then forget.

After a sock is darned
dark thread remains to scar
the heel
raised as a new wound.
With every step, a foot
recalls the tearing of the wool.
        memory inhabits
the slipstitch and the knot,
no matter how skilled
the seamstress, her fingers
made for repairing the grief
in a torn black shirt,
or the pants split apart
like a fissured pair of souls.

PART FOUR

In my mother's kitchen,
there was no Maimonides,
only a woman's guide
to the farklempt—
        tears we wept
into the tea so that the leaves
might taste of   salt.
We chopped our fingertips
into the tsimmes pot
knowing the meal demands
an injury that will not heal.
        Mamme said
Best to slice your wrist
before the sacrifice
is asked. We kneaded bread
so deep our palms turned blue
with bruises   too hard
as though we hoped
to shape a second husband
from the dough, a second father,
a man more pliable
beneath our gentling hands.

Last night my pillow broke
into a thousand feathers.
My mouth gave birth to wings
          but crippled ones,
as if a child had struck
a white stork from the sky,
his slingshot made for killing
what is only beautiful beyond
our gravity   our pull.
He left the bird for dead
beneath my tongue. I felt
the needle of its beak,
its pinions gray as fever,
its claws   unholy thorns

The outside world is treyf
and, therefore, beautiful
for all I cannot eat of it.
                  two words that taste
forbidden in my mouth:
devouring and *satiate*.
Some landscapes that I want
to try: a valley
curving like a cloven hoof,
the clammish sea,
                  cities where
one language bleeds
into the next, where crowds
are winged and swarming
things, and every touch
the idolatry of wine.

The laws command
a linearity of gaze
    although our eyes
want to slide like water
down a cambered surface
(a belly newly bathed,
a breast), our eyes
desiring rounded things,
apples so pregnant
we can't resist their juice.
Of course Eve ate
when she was offered,
      palmed the fruit,
familiar as the weight
of her own body.
       she bit
into the last good flesh
of Eden, her teeth
incising there a line
shaped like a smile,
and in her mouth
a questioning, a tongue
made heretic.

After such modesty,
how did I turn to pollen
carried everywhere?
Each part of me went yellow—
        my yellow feet
my knees   my elbows yellow
my yellow lips   my eyes
        this dust of yellowness
that is my fingerprint.
Where did I throw my dress
composed of shadows?
My stockings? The scarf
that covered up my hair?
No one can look away
from a blossoming like mine.
No one can explicate
the sudden birth of stigma
        anther and the ovary,
the golden particles
of touch I leave behind.

[version one]

I began in modesty but turned
to pollen in my sleep—
          and how my feet
glowed yellow,
my sharpest yellow points,
my yellow openings   my eyes,
        this brush of yellowness
that is each fingertip. After
such modesty, what happened
to the shadow of my dress?
What became   the coverings?
Even my lover can't look
beyond the blossom.
He can't explain the petals
          that grow inside of me,
the gilded sand that covers
every surface when we wake.

[version two]

What need for modesty
when I am pollen everywhere?
—all my edges yellow,
my yellow palms and feet
and this my yellowness,
the words I scatter, the touch
of hands. I dropped my dress,
undid the hooks and stays
that held me in. I ripped
the covering from my hair.
I am the anther and the ovary,
the liturgy, the illustrator's gold,
the flower painted in the pages
of the sacred book

[version three]

My smile has gone missing
in the Pale of Settlement.
It wanders the dusty roads
                a peddler
weighed down with sacks
of cloth and trinkets
that nobody wants to own.
Children throw stones
                You dirty smile,
they scream and run away.
Their laughter cuts
deep notches through
the air.
                In the country,
such cruelty is common
as burying a child,
easy as snapping
a chicken's neck.
I have misplaced the knack
of ecstasy, dropped it
while wandering a field,
left for gleaners to find,
their bodies bent
to pick the shining object
from the soil—this scrap
of treasure, this trash.

Consider the present
for my mother, a carp
wrapped in white paper
    tied with twine—
                it held
a poem too,
            she never read
my fish scale sentences,
my dorsal nouns   verbs
that push through water
like a fin, my phrases
boney-sharp as spines,
        soaked with sea.
They must have stunk
the kitchen,
until she tossed them out
to be a feast for alley cats,
        starved
enough to eat the flesh
and rotten savories
of words.

                        [version one]

63

That carp
I gave my mother,
choking in paper,
        bound with rope—
                it held
a poem in its mouth.
If only she had read
the sentences like scales,
the nouns   the verbs
that fin through water,
the boney spines.
If only she had kept
the words,
but threw them out
to feed the feral cats
who stalk the alleyway,
        so hungry
they chewed the flesh,
the verse that stank
of rot.

                        [version two]

In a woman's life,
all lists become her poetry,
so that a recipe for cake
is just the verse form
of desire

       honey dripped in lines
and cups of flour, white
as fancy paper.
She makes an inventory
of her household goods,
each fork   each kosher plate
a liturgy that praises
appetite   restrained,
songs rendered into shards.
She is the psalmist David
in her chores (sing *hallelujah*
to the cotton sheets that flap
the wind like pages
of an open book)

       (sing *hallelujah*
to the kitchen floor,
a miracle of words beneath
its mud) (sing *hallelujah*
to the windows washed —
how crystalline the glass,
the panes   breakable,
transparent as the soul)

How can I rest inside
the old intimacy
of this body?
My neck betrays itself
with the smell of dying
roses. I was petals once,
although I hated
my fragility,   breasts
too easily fingered,
crushed beneath a hand.

        Somewhere
there stands a vase
brimming stagnant water,
green film across
the surface of the glass.
Someone should break
the vessel—better
the ecstasy of shards,
than (slowly)   (slowly)
giving way to rot.

All cooking brings a death
to its ingredients
an alchemy that promises
eternal taste, although
a life must be consumed
before it spoils. Know this—
I'm steeped in prophesy,
my visions   silver fish
herrings sunk in brine.
Now the peppercorn
becomes a tarnished berry,
now the onion is encased
in a pearled sheen
to make all women weep,
now lemons are luminous
as paste, bright yellow jewels
that imitate citrines.

O dearest one, O pebble
in my throat, I am returned
to the fever-world—
my rooms made empty now,
my hearth so cold so very cold,
my window-eyes destroyed.
I should have known
these hands are temporary arts
of river mud
I should have known
there never was a blood
to paint the lintel, the Angel
entering through every door
of me. Why wish for ice,
when ice comes soon enough?
the fever-world a blessing
on this   decrepit house
we call a body, the fever-world
a nail pulled from the wall,
the dovetail snapped in two,
and all the falling down
that follows after.

Translator's Note

After so many years spent in her company, I feel certain that Ida Lewin (or someone like her) existed in the imaginary Polish town of AlwaysWinter. Maybe she was born in 1906. She wrote of a sealed world with its own mythology—cursed children, omens flying on black wings, poisoned fruit. She recorded an ever-modernizing landscape of trolley cars, café philosophers, and illicit love affairs.

I think she had the gift of Sight. Too many of her poems prophesy a darkness spreading across the countryside, a thick fog that clung to the ankles, preventing action and escape.

She died in 1938, during a flu epidemic that killed thirty-one other Jews in AlwaysWinter, including her only child, a baby girl named Rivka. In 1986, two schoolchildren discovered her manuscripts as well as diaries, accounting ledgers, and a handmade book of kosher recipes, buried in a metal sewing tin behind the former site of the Great Synagogue. A sheaf of over fifty crumpled pages might be all that remains of Ida's poetry.

As for translators, we were slow to address her work, poems both pleasure and challenge, scented with spices. Ida scribbled in the margins of newspapers, on the backs of used envelopes, and alongside old shopping lists folded and refolded into permanent creases. We only have these porous documents and her spectral, gauzy words. What remains? What have insects eaten from the page? What has rain washed away?

– J.I.D.

ACKNOWLEDGEMENTS

Each poem was published under the title "Fragment from a Nonexistent Yiddish Poet."

II – [On Rosh Hashanah, I try]
32 Poems – [Each year the chill creeps in] and
    [To translate ripened fruit]
Anti – [I think she must be Death] and
    [In the city of machines]
Barn Owl Review – [In the fever-world, my dearest]
Bateau – [After fasting I'm thinner than]
Blackbird – [to be studied, the way],
    [I believe in the body's power],
    [If beets complain, they say], and
    [I have swaddled he baby]
DIAGRAM – [The missing child won't]
Drunken Boat – [At Purim, an angel dances],
    [winters in Poland] both versions, and
    [I dream the myth of men]
Fringe – [I am like the fire],
    [I've heard that Polish wives cook beets],
    [Once I held a painted miniature], and
    [I watch the Polish women sell]
In Posse Review – [forewarned, we spent the night]
Kritya – [We've heard the ash-bird],
    [Before the wedding, a bride unveils],
    [Not every woman needs], [remember my fingertips?],
    [This country is a dollhouse],
    [In a woman's life], and
    [How can I rest inside]
Linebreak – [My mind grew quiet]
New Vilna Review – [Last night my pillow broke] and
    [The outside world is treyf]
Nextbook – [Those women who sit shiva],
    [Someday we'll say], [After such modesty] version one,
    [My smile has gone missing]
Ninth Letter – [In my mother's kitchen]
Saranac Review – [Dear one, I saw it in a dream]
Sawbuck – [Tonight I am remembering],
    [Some claimed] all three versions,
    [I've heard it said], and [After a sock is darned]
Siren – [Someone has seen the bird again],
    [little boots little boots], [I cursed my body],
    [I come back from the bath], and [late summertime]
Subtropics – [O dearest one, O pebble]

THANKS

This book was made possible by funds granted to the author through a Sosland Foundation Fellowship at the Center for Advanced Holocaust Studies, United States Holocaust Memorial Museum. The statements made and views expressed, however, are solely the responsibility of the author.

*

I am extremely grateful for the support of the Center for Advanced Holocaust Studies, the Virginia Center for the Creative Arts, and the University of Nebraska-Lincoln.

I also want to thank the people who have cheered me on during the writing of this book: Jennifer Hansen, Leslie Harrison, Kristin Naca, April Ossmann, Hilda Raz, Vincent Slatt, Yerra Sugarman. And thank you to Brandel France de Bravo, Patric Pepper, and Carly Sachs of the Washington Writers' Publishing House—wonderful editors, champions of poetry, and dear friends.

Finally, my love and thanks to my parents, Jeannette and Stephen Dubrow, to my brother The Schmer, and to my puppy Argos. And to my husband Jeremy, I love you in the whole wide world.

About the Poet

Jehanne Dubrow was born in Italy and grew up in Yugoslavia, Zaire, Poland, Belgium, Austria, and the United States. She earned her PhD in English from the University of Nebraska-Lincoln and her MFA in poetry from the University of Maryland, College Park. Her work has appeared in *Poetry*, *Prairie Schooner*, *The New England Review*, *Barrow Street*, *Gulf Coast*, and *Shenandoah*. She is the author of a poetry collection, *The Hardship Post*, and a chapbook, *The Promised Bride*. A third collection of poetry, *Stateside*, will be published by Northwestern University Press in 2010. She is an assistant professor in creative writing and literature at Washington College.

About Washington Writers' Publishing House

Washington Writers' Publishing House is a non-profit organization that has published over 50 volumes of poetry since 1973 and so far nearly a dozen volumes of fiction. The press sponsors an annual competition for poets and fiction writers living in the Washington-Baltimore area.

WWPH has received grants from the Lannan Foundation, the National Endowment for the Arts, the DC Commission on the Arts and Humanities, the Nation magazine, and the Poetry Society of America. Many individuals have also assisted, encouraged, and supported our work through the years.

Become an Author

Submit your book-length poetry or fiction manuscripts to Washington Writers' Publishing House's annual poetry and fiction competitions. Visit our web site at www.washingtonwriters.org for contest guidelines.

Recent Titles

Poetry:
From the Fever-World, by Jehanne Dubrow
Provenance, by Brandel France de Bravo
Mystery Schools, by Bruce MacKinnon
the steam sequence, by Carly Sachs
Temporary Apprehensions, by Patric Pepper
Gagarin Street, by Piotr Gwiazda
Cleave, by Moira Egan

Fiction:
Calvin, by William Littlejohn
Success: Stories, by David A. Taylor
And Silent Left the Place, by Elizabeth Bruce
Nora's Army, by Dennis Collins
Can't Remember Playing, by Gretchen Roberts
Tin Mines and Concubines, by Hilary Tham

To order these books or other WWPH titles visit us at www.washingtonwriters.org or e-mail us at wwphpress@gmail.com. Books may also be ordered on the web through Small Press Distribution at www.spdbooks.org and though Amazon at www.amazon.com.

Colophon

The text and display typeface is Palatino Linotype, a digitized version of the mid-20th century typeface Palatino, known for its solidity and legibility. Named after Giambattista Palatino, a master of calligraphy during the 16th century, Palatino has itself become a modern classic. The book design and composition is by Patric Pepper. The cover design concept is by Alex Castro and the author, Jehanne Dubrow. The final cover design and layout is by Kathy Keler. The map, "Always Winter, 1903" was drawn by the author, Jehanne Dubrow. The cover art is by the artist ©lauren e. simonutti, who wishes her name to appear as printed here. The author's photograph is by Jeremy Schaub. This book was printed in the United States of America by Lightning Source, Inc.